Bears and
Pandas

CONTENTS

© Aladdin Books Ltd

Designed and produced by
Aladdin Books Ltd
70 Old Compton Street
London W1

First published in the
United States in 1986 by
Gloucester Press
387 Park Avenue South
New York NY 10016

Printed in Belgium

ISBN 0-531-17026-8

Library of Congress
Catalog Card No. 86-80622

*Certain illustrations have previously appeared in the "Closer Look"
series published by Gloucester Press.*

A CLOSER LOOK AT

Bears and Pandas

BIBBY WHITTAKER

Illustrated by
RICHARD ORR,
KAREN JOHNSON AND DAVID ASHBY

Consultant
DAPHNE HILLS

Gloucester Press
New York · Toronto · 1986

Understanding bears

Bears and pandas may look playful and amusing, tumbling down a snowy hillside or lumbering along in their pigeon-toed style. In reality, however, they tend to be shy animals and can be extremely dangerous. Bears and pandas are unpredictable, and we do not know as much about them as we would like.

Some of this mystery about bears and pandas is due to the fact that they are so hard to study. They lead very solitary lives and bears in particular are extremely variable in appearance and behavior.

Bear ancestors

Bears evolved from an early creature that was like a cross between a raccoon and a jackal. Over millions of years, its descendants developed into the first true bears, which were much smaller than modern bears.

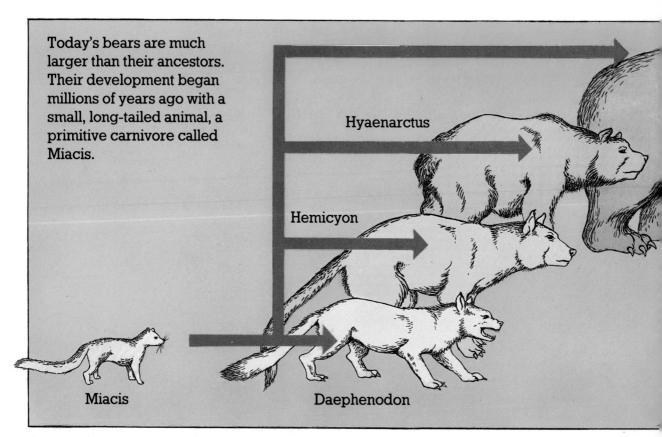

Today's bears are much larger than their ancestors. Their development began millions of years ago with a small, long-tailed animal, a primitive carnivore called Miacis.

Hyaenarctus

Hemicyon

Miacis

Daephenodon

Many bears have poor eyesight and hearing. However, with their long snouts, they all have a very good sense of smell. This helps them find food and warns them of danger.

Ursus (10 million years ago)

One of the descendants of this animal was a doglike creature, which eventually gave rise to the first true bears, about fifteen million years ago.

Bears and pandas

Pandas and bears are mammals. This means the females have special glands that make milk to feed the cubs. They are carnivores, or meat-eaters. However, their choice of food depends on what is available, so they have become omnivorous – eating both meat and vegetation.

The pandas

Until recently, scientists have been in doubt as to whether bears and pandas belonged to the same animal family. Some scientists believed that the Red panda was related to the raccoon family. Like raccoons, they spend most of their lives in trees, and usually live in groups of three or more. The other type of panda, the Giant panda, is more obviously bear-like, both in behavior and appearance. You can read more about the Giant panda later in this book.

The Red panda has several raccoon-like features. Because of this, many scientists once believed that both pandas belonged to the raccoon family.

Raccoon

Giant panda

Red panda

These are the seven species of bears.

American Black bear

Spectacled bear

Asian Black bear

Sloth bear

Sun bear

Brown bear

Polar bear

The bears

There are seven species, or kinds, of bears and most of them live in the Northern Hemisphere. The bear species have much more in common than the two pandas have, but there are also differences, both in the way they look and the way they behave. Some of these variations are due to bears' great ability to adapt to their surroundings.

The thickness and texture of bears' fur varies from one kind to another. The color of the fur is even more inconsistent – sometimes even within one species. This is why there were once thought to be over 200 different kinds of bears.

The Latin name for this bear reflects its fearsome appearance (*Ursus horribilis*), but "grizzly" refers to its gray-tipped, brown fur.

8

Brown bears

Brown bears once ranged in huge numbers across Britain, Europe, Asia and western North America. Although they have disappeared from many countries, they still can be found in more parts of the world than any other bears.

(light gray)	Brown bear
(dark gray)	Grizzly bear
(black)	Himalayan Brown bear
(white)	Blue bear
(gray)	Syrian bear

A coat of many colors

Despite their name, Brown bears are not necessarily brown. Their coats can be cream, brown, gray or almost black, depending on where they live. Those living in dense forests have dark, coarse fur that blends in well with their surroundings. Brown bears living in the open tend to have lighter, softer fur.

These are all members of the Brown bear family. At 2.7 m (9 ft) tall, the Alaskan Kodiak bear is the largest land carnivore in the world.

Kodiak bear

Blue bear

Syrian bear   Himalayan Brown bear

Brown bear

9

Searching for food

When food supplies are plentiful, bears may gather together to feed. Usually, however, bears need large individual "territories" in which to feed.

Bears define their territories with scent marks and scratches on the tree bark. The higher the scratches on a tree, the less likely other bears will trespass, since the height of the scratches will be an indication of the bear's size.

The huge Brown bears of Alaska and British Columbia probably owe their size to their high-protein salmon diet. The older, dominant bears claim the best fishing areas for themselves.

Thorough feeders

Insects, roots, fruit, honey and carrion, or dead animals – all of these and more make up a bear's diet. Black bears are better suited to climbing trees than the heavy Brown bears, so their meals often include pine cones, nuts and even wasps' nests. Bears are expert diggers and will use their strong claws to capture small animals living underground.

The yearly cycle

Mother bears are fiercely protective of their cubs. Even so, many cubs are killed by predators and even adult male bears may attack and eat them.

Late spring is the breeding season for bears. Because bears do not live in groups, the males must find the females to mate with them. They do this by following the scent marks on the trees.

In the summer, when food is most plentiful, bears eat huge quantities in order to build up a thick layer of fat. Their bodies then live off this fat during the winter months of hibernation. For the females, this is especially important because this is the time when the cubs are born.

Mothers and cubs

While dozing in her den, the mother gives birth to up to three cubs. The cubs are blind, toothless and almost hairless when born. Brown bear cubs weigh 0.5 kg (1 lb) and Black bear cubs are even smaller.

The mother bear remains in the den with her cubs until spring. Until then, the cubs' only food is milk from their mother.

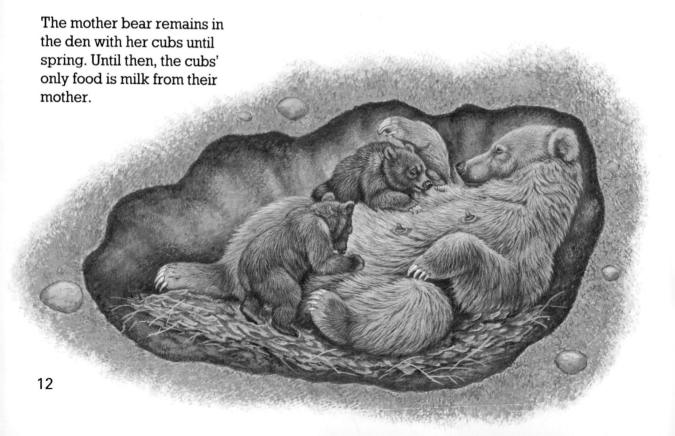

In October, bears find a sheltered place in which to hibernate. It may be a cave, or simply a hollowed out spot under tree roots. Bears often return to the same den year after year.

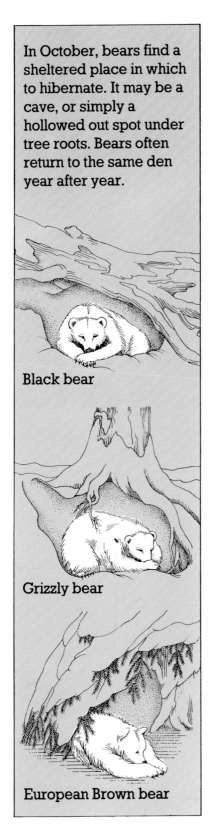

Black bear

Grizzly bear

European Brown bear

The mother bear "talks" to her cubs with grunting sounds, to make sure that they follow her as she searches for food.

Black bears

In North America, the distribution of Brown bears overlaps with that of the American Black bears. The Black bears are the smaller species, growing to about 1.5 m (5 ft) tall. Like Brown bears, their name is misleading, and the color of their fur can be dark brown, cinnamon brown, cream, blue-black or black. Even cubs in the same litter may vary in color.

Black bears once lived in nearly all the woodlands of North America, but their numbers are now much smaller.

Fast bears

Black bears are very strong and fast. They can run up to 48 k/h (30 mph) – a surprising feat considering the bears' bulky build.

American Black bear

Black bears will eat almost any vegetation – bulbs, grass, herbs and clover, for instance. They also eat some unusual things like briers. Black bears are especially fond of anything sweet, such as berries.

14

Although different in color, these are both American Black bears. Only their straighter backs, smaller size and pale, upturned noses help to distinguish them from Brown bears.

15

Staking a claim

The Black bear's forest home provides a wide variety of food. One treat to be found in trees is a termites' nest. The bear tears at the wood with its claws and licks the swarming insects from its paw.

Other non-vegetarian meals may include small rodents, like mice and voles, as well as frogs, fish and eggs. They will also attack and eat any wounded or sick animal.

Funny but dangerous

Many North American Black bears live in National Parks. Some have lost their natural fear of humans and will stand up on their back legs, comically begging for food from people in cars. But visitors to the parks are told not to feed them and to keep their windows closed. Black bears can be unpredictable and have attacked and injured people who came too close.

Bears will do almost anything to get honey. They tear open the bees' nest with their sharp claws. Perhaps the bears' thick fur protects them from the stings, since they seem to ignore them.

Asiatic Black bears
have been known to kill
sheep and calves.

Asiatic Black bear

The Asiatic Black bear is also known as the
Himalayan or Moon bear. This is the only
species of bear in which the male lives with
the family. These bears can grow to a length
of 1.5 m (5 ft), and they are good climbers.
They hibernate high up in the hollows of
trees, and it is here that the females give birth
to the cubs. Asiatic Black bears eat fruit,
insects and small animals.

The fur markings on an Asiatic Black bear
are very distinctive. There is a V-shaped
white mark on the chest and the upper lip is
often white. The claws are small and black.

Asiatic Black bear

Polar bears

Polar bear

The Polar bear is probably the easiest bear to identify. Its white fur acts as an effective camouflage, or disguise, in the Polar bear's Arctic home of snow and pack-ice. Here, very few plants can survive, so for much of the year the Polar bear must hunt for prey.

True predators

Most other bears survive mainly on vegetation, but Polar bears are, by necessity, mostly carnivorous. They are true predators – animals that survive by hunting and killing other animals. Polar bears have developed many features to become expert Arctic hunters.

The Ice bear's weapons

A Polar bear's body is well-adapted to life in the water and on ice. In addition to its long, white oily fur, a Polar bear has a streamlined shape for swimming. Compared to most other bear species, its neck and body are longer, and its head is smaller.

A Polar bear's rump is set higher than its shoulders. This helps it to run fast. Its huge clawed feet have more fur on the soles than those of other bears. The fur protects the skin from the freezing cold of the ice and water. It also gives the Polar bear a good grip on the icy surface.

Polar bears are nearly as large as the huge Kodiak Brown bears. An average adult male measures 2.4 m (7.75 ft) from nose to tail, and weighs 400 kg (880 lb), but much heavier Polar bears are common.

Food in the Arctic

During the Arctic summer Polar bears may wander inland, where they can enjoy a more omnivorous diet of birds' eggs, berries and lichen. They have also been seen foraging in garbage dumps near Arctic settlements, as well as feeding on whale and other carcasses on shore. But the Arctic summer is brief, so Polar bears are most often found on the ice. It is here that they hunt seals.

The future "Water bear?"

A lot of a Polar bear's time is spent in the water. This has caused the Polar bear to develop several features unique in the bear family. It can close its nostrils and keep its eyes open under water. When swimming, a Polar bear does not use its back legs to kick like other land animals. Instead it uses them like a rudder. A Polar bear's front feet are slightly webbed.

Some scientists believe that these developments show that Polar bears are evolving into sea mammals. But evolution is a very slow process. It will be millions of years, if at all, before Polar bears fully become sea-dwelling animals.

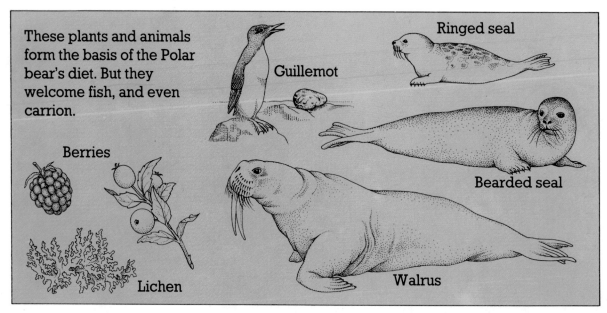

These plants and animals form the basis of the Polar bear's diet. But they welcome fish, and even carrion.

Guillemot

Ringed seal

Bearded seal

Berries

Lichen

Walrus

The Polar bear's chief prey is the Ringed seal. Seals need air to breathe and in the winter they make holes in the ice. When they appear, the Polar bear attacks.

Female seals den up under the ice in the winter and give birth to their pups. But even here they aren't safe from the bears. With their long sharp claws, Polar bears can dig through the snow and ice.

21

Learning to hunt

While other species of female bears introduce their cubs to the food of the forests, Polar bear mothers must show their cubs how to hunt. There are many skills the cubs must acquire, by following her example.

Polar bears are expert swimmers, but seals are better. So Polar bears have developed other tactics to catch their prey.

The hunter's disguise

Nearly invisible in its white fur, a Polar bear will creep, with its body flattened, across the ice and snow toward a seal. The bear may cover its black nose with its paw to hide it. Once near enough, the Polar bear rushes forward and kills the seal.

Polar bear cubs spend two years with their mother, learning the skills of hunting.

As winter nears, the female Polar bear digs a large den under the land ice. In about December, the cubs are born. They will remain in the den until spring, nestling in the mother's warm fur. When the cubs leave the den, the mother must protect them from hungry male bears.

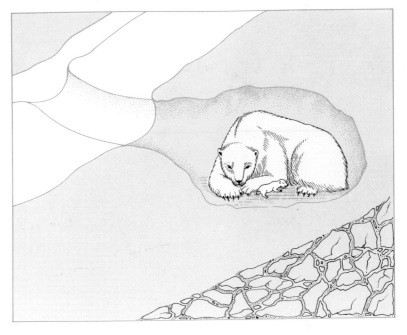

The nocturnal bears

The Spectacled, or Andean, bear is the only South American bear. An agile climber, this mostly vegetarian bear spends much of its time feeding in trees, climbing to heights of up to 30 m (100 ft) in search of food.

The 1.2 m (4 ft) Sun bear of southern Asia is the smallest of the bears. It spends more time in trees than other bears and the soles of its feet are hairless, enabling it to climb well. The cubs, usually two, are born on the ground, well-hidden in the thick undergrowth of the forest floor.

Deadly panic

The Sloth bear of India and Ceylon has very poor vision and hearing. Because of this, it is easily startled, and will often attack and kill in a panic.

The Spectacled bear's name comes from the fur markings around its eyes. There is such variation in these markings that no two Spectacled bears look exactly alike.

With their nostrils sealed, Sloth bears push their heads into termites' nests, blow away the dust and suck up the insects.

Sloth bear
Sun bear

Because of its great
fondness for honey, the Sun
bear is also known as the
Honey bear.

The Giant panda became the symbol for the World Wildlife Fund in 1961.

Like bears, Giant pandas leave scent marks to define their territories.

The pandas

The 1.5 m (5 ft) Giant panda once ranged widely across China, but today it is only found in one part of western China. Its home is in the damp bamboo forests that grow high up in the mountains. The small, cat-like Red panda is also found here, but its home extends further westward to the Himalayas.

Pandas discovered

Until the middle of the 19th century, pandas were unknown outside China.

Dying bamboo

Bamboo is the Giant panda's main source of food, so life in the dense bamboo forests would seem to provide all that pandas could need. But each kind of bamboo lives for only a certain number of years before it flowers and dies – and then whole forests suddenly vanish.

When this happened in 1975, 150 pandas may have died of starvation. Only about 1,000 pandas are still alive.

Red panda
Giant panda

Giant pandas

Pandas are active throughout the day and night, alternately feeding and sleeping. An adult panda will eat about 15 kg (33 lb) of bamboo daily – or over 6 tons per year. Pandas must consume such enormous quantities because they do not digest the bamboo well and gain little nourishment from it. It is difficult for pandas to catch other animals to eat, but they enjoy any carrion they find.

Giant panda cubs

Panda cubs are usually born in September. At birth they measure about 10 cm (4 in) and weigh 142 gm (5 oz). This is 800 times lighter than the mother panda. But they grow quickly and within nine months the cubs will weigh 27 kg (60 lb). Female pandas only raise one cub every two years, and not all of these survive. For an endangered species this is a real disadvantage.

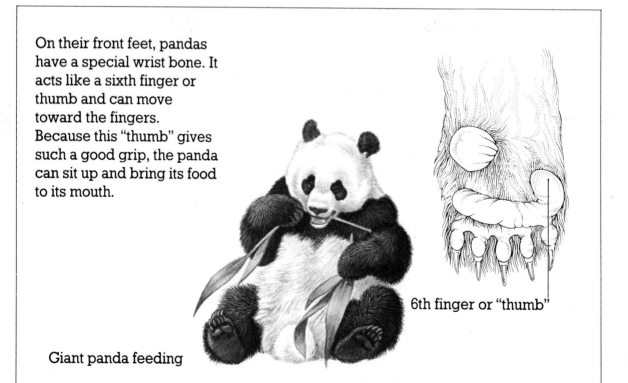

On their front feet, pandas have a special wrist bone. It acts like a sixth finger or thumb and can move toward the fingers. Because this "thumb" gives such a good grip, the panda can sit up and bring its food to its mouth.

Giant panda feeding

6th finger or "thumb"

Panda cubs are usually born in a den. This may be in a tree hollow or under overhanging rocks. The cubs are blind and toothless when they are born.

Saving bears and pandas

Bears and pandas have few enemies other than human beings. In the past, the danger from humans was twofold. The ever-growing world population needed more land on which to settle and to grow food. This in turn greatly reduced the once vast habitats of bears and pandas. Large animals like these need large areas in which to feed, so many starved. Others were hunted by humans, either to protect their settlements from the dangerous animals or simply for the sport.

The future for bears

There could never be as many bears, living in as many parts of the world, as there once were. However, several international conservation groups are now working together to keep the numbers of bears from dropping further. For example, all of the countries within the Arctic region have now restricted the hunting of Polar bears in order to prevent their extinction.

Other bears and their remaining forest homes are not yet fully protected. Until they are, the work of conservationists can only have a limited success.

In recent years, people have become much more aware of the importance of conservation. Perhaps in the future, humans will become the allies, instead of the enemies, of bears and pandas.

Protected pandas

A great deal has been done already to protect the Giant panda. It is against the law in China to hunt pandas – or even to hurt one. Pandas may not be sold, although they are sometimes given to zoos in other countries. Before long, there will be another bamboo "die-off." It is hoped that research now being done by China and the World Wildlife Fund will prevent more pandas from dying of starvation.

Glossary

Camouflage   Disguise of color or patterns that hides an animal.

Carnivore   Animal that eats meat.

Conservation   Protection of natural resources and animal life.

Evolution   Development of a species from its original form to its present form.

Habitat   An animal's natural home.

Hibernation   Winter sleep when an animal's temperature lowers and heartbeat slows. In bears this change is limited and they can easily awaken.

Mammals   Group of animals that are usually covered in fur, and in which the females have milk glands.

Nocturnal   Active during the night.

Omnivore   Animal that eats both meat and vegetation.

Predator   Animal that hunts and kills other animals for food.

Prey   Animal that is hunted or killed and eaten by a predator.

Territory   Area of land in which a bear eats and lives, and which it defends against other bears.

Index

PRINTED IN BELGIUM BY
proost
INTERNATIONAL BOOK PRODUCTION